I've Got a Poem For You

Poems to Perform

Collected by John Foster

Illustrated by
Belle Mellor

OXFORD
UNIVERSITY PRESS

OXFORD
UNIVERSITY PRESS

Great Clarendon Street, Oxford OX2 6DP

Oxford University Press is a department of the University of Oxford.
It furthers the University's objective of excellence in research, scholarship,
and education by publishing worldwide in

Oxford   New York

Auckland   Cape Town   Dar es Salaam   Hong Kong   Karachi
Kuala Lumpur   Madrid   Melbourne   Mexico City   Nairobi
New Delhi   Shanghai   Taipei   Toronto

With offices in

Argentina   Austria   Brazil   Chile   Czech Republic   France   Greece
Guatemala   Hungary   Italy   Japan   Poland   Portugal   Singapore
South Korea   Switzerland   Thailand   Turkey   Ukraine   Vietnam

Oxford is a registered trade mark of Oxford University Press
in the UK and in certain other countries

British Library Cataloguing in Publication Data available

ISBN-13: 978-0-19-276256-6
ISBN-10: 0-19-276256-7

3 5 7 9 10 8 6 4

Typeset by Mary Tudge (Typesetting Services)

Printed in the UK by Cox & Wyman Ltd, Reading, Berkshire

Contents

Song of the Wizard's Imp

Catch me if you can,
I'm a whisper of air,
a splinter of sunlight
that's gone if you stare.

Catch me if you can,
I'm a shadowy patch,
a rustle of cobweb
that's gone if you snatch.

Catch me if you can,
but be sure that you dare,
for I nestle to rest
in a wizard's warm hair.

Yes, catch me if you can,
but be warned I am weird,
for I settle to sleep
in the wizard's white beard.

Oh, catch me if you can,
but don't wake the wizard.
He'll glare and he'll growl
and you'll end up a lizard.

Tony Mitton

Anancy

Anancy is a spider;
Anancy is a man;
Anancy's West Indian
And West African.

Sometimes, he wears a waistcoat;
Sometimes, he carries a cane;
Sometimes, he sports a top-hat;
Sometimes, he's just a plain
Ordinary, black, hairy spider.

Anancy is vastly cunning,
Tremendously greedy,
Excessively charming,
Hopelessly dishonest,
Warmly loving,
Firmly confident,
Fiercely wild,
A fabulous character,
Completely out of our mind
And out of his, too.

Anancy is a master planner,
A great user
Of other people's plans;
He pockets everybody's food,
Shelter, land, money, and more;
He achieves mountains of things,
Like stolen flour dumplings;
He deceives millions of people,
Even the man in the moon;
And he solves all the mysteries
On earth, in air, under sea.

And always,
Anancy changes
From a spider into a man
And from a man into a spider
And back again
At the drop of a sleepy eyelid.

Andrew Salkey

Mang, Katong, and the Crocodile King

Deep in the jungle,
in the land of Mangoree,
lived Mang, the magic drummer,
in a frangipani tree.
Boom-kiri, boom-kiri, boom-boom-kiree.

A boy called Katong
from the village, came to sing,
'Mang, make your magic
melt the Crocodile King.'
Boom-kiri, boom-kiri, boom-boom-karing.

'The Crocodile King
has eaten my ma,
chewed up my gran
and swallowed my pa.'
Boom-kiri, boom-kiri, boom-boom-karaa.

'You are small,' said Mang,
'but you want a great thing.
It will be hard to melt
the Crocodile King.'
Boom-kiri, boom-kiri, boom-boom-karing.

'I will help,' said Katong.
And he beat on the drum
while Mang made his magic,
'Basoko, bagum.'
Boom-kiri, boom-kiri, boom-boom-katum.

Then sparks flew up
from their beating hands
and went whizzing and sizzling
all over the land,
like fireworks made
from the sun and moon,
until they lit up King Croc
in the village lagoon.
Boom-kiri, boom-kiri, boom-boom-boom.

The villagers cheered,
'Hooray! hooray!'
as they saw the sparks melt
King Crocodile away.
Boom-kiri, boom-kiri, boom-boom-kiray.

'He's gone,' cried Katong.
'Now my village is free!'
And Mang said, 'Katong,
come and live with me.
We'll both make magic
in my frangipani tree,
deep in the jungle
in the land of Mangoree.'
Boom-kiri, boom-kiri, boom-boom-karee.

Jennifer Tweedie

The Hippopotamus Song

A bold Hippopotamus was standing one day
On the banks of the cool Shalimar.
He gazed at the bottom as it peacefully lay
By the light of the evening star.
Away on a hilltop sat combing her hair
His fair Hippopotamine maid;
The Hippopotamus was no ignoramus
And sang her this sweet serenade.

> Mud, mud, glorious mud,
> Nothing quite like it for cooling the
>   blood!
> So follow me, follow,
> Down to the hollow
> And there let us wallow
> In glorious mud!

The fair Hippopotama he aimed to entice
From her seat on that hilltop above,
As she hadn't got a ma to give her advice,
Came tiptoeing down to her love.
Like thunder the forest re-echoed the sound
Of the song that they sang as they met.
His inamorata adjusted her garter
And lifted her voice in duet.

Mud, mud, glorious mud,
Nothing quite like it for cooling the
  blood!
So follow me, follow,
Down to the hollow
And there let us wallow
In glorious mud!

Now more Hippopotami began to convene
On the banks of that river so wide.
I wonder now what am I to say of the scene
That ensued by the Shalimar side?
They dived all at once with an ear-splitting
  splosh
Then rose to the surface again,
A regular army of Hippopotami
All singing this haunting refrain.

Mud, mud, glorious mud,
Nothing quite like it for cooling the
  blood!
So follow me, follow,
Down to the hollow
And there let us wallow
In glorious mud!

Michael Flanders

The House of the Tiger

This is the jungle, the house of the tiger.
This is the dawn
That breaks the night
And brings the light
That wakes the house of the tiger.

This is the tree of bark and thorn
All dressed in the mists of early dawn
That breaks the night
That brings the light
That wakes the house of the tiger.

This is the tiger of tiger born
Who hid in the tree of bark and thorn
All dressed in the mists of early dawn
That breaks the night
That brings the light
That wakes the house of the tiger.

This is the antelope hoof and horn
That passed the tiger of tiger born
Who hid in the tree of bark and thorn
All dressed in the mists of early dawn
That breaks the night
That brings the light
That wakes the house of the tiger.

This is the crow who crowed to warn
The antelope of hoof and horn
To run from the tiger of tiger born
Who leaped from the tree of bark and thorn
All dressed in the mists of early dawn
That breaks the night
That brings the light
That wakes the house of the tiger.

This is the monkey of chatter and scorn
Who cheered the crow who crowed to warn
The antelope of hoof and horn
Who escaped the tiger of tiger born
Roaring under the tree of bark and thorn
All dressed in the mists of early dawn
That breaks the night
That brings the light
That has woken the house of the tiger.

Julie Holder

The Newcomer

'There's something new in the river,'
The fish said as it swam—
'It's got no scales, no fins, and no gills,
And ignores the impassable dam.'

'There's something new in the trees,'
I heard a bloated thrush sing,
'It's got no beak, no claws, and no feathers,
And not even the ghost of a wing.'

'There's something new in the warren,'
Said the rabbit to the doe.
'It's got no fur, no eyes, and no paws,
Yet digs deeper than we dare go.'

'There's something new in the whiteness,'
Said the snow-bright polar bear.
'I saw its shadow on a glacier,
But it left no pawmarks there.'

Through the animal kingdom
The news was spreading fast—
No beak, no claws, no feather,
No scales, no fur, no gills,
It lives in the trees and the water,
In the soil and the snow and the hills,
And it kills and it kills and it kills.

Brian Patten

The Spiders Cast Their Spell

Break our
web
Break our
universe

    We in return
    will bless you
    with a curse

May your two legs
grow to be eight

    May your sleep be
    too light
    for the weight
    of your dreams

May your house
collapse
at the slight
touch of a breeze

And as you sit
among the ruin
of your memories

May you wish
for thread to spin
May you wish
for thread to spin

John Agard

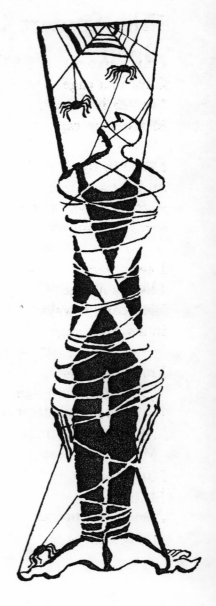

I'm a Parrot

I am a parrot
I live in a cage
I'm nearly always
in a vex-up rage

I used to fly
all light and free
in the luscious green
forest canopy

I am a parrot
I live in a cage
I'm nearly always
in a vex-up rage

I miss the wind
against my wing
I miss the nut
and the fruit picking

I am a parrot
I live in a cage
I'm nearly always
in a vex-up rage

I squawk I talk
I curse I swear
I repeat the things
I shouldn't hear

So don't come near me
or put out your hand
because I'll pick you
if I can
pickyou
pickyou
if I can

I want to be Free
Can't You Understand

Grace Nichols

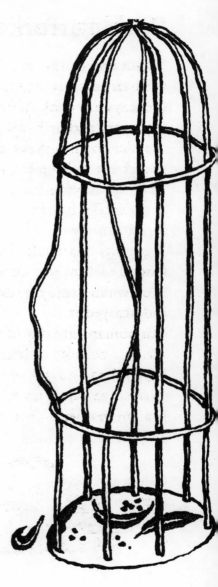

20

Talking Turkeys!!

Be nice to yu turkeys dis christmas
Cos turkeys jus wanna hav fun
Turkeys are cool, turkeys are wicked
An every turkey has a Mum.
Be nice to yu turkeys dis christmas,
Don't eat it, keep it alive,
It could be yu mate an not on yu plate
Say, Yo! Turkey I'm on your side.

I got lots of friends who are turkeys
An all of dem fear christmas time,
Dey wanna enjoy it, dey say humans
  destroyed it
An humans are out of dere mind,
Yeah, I got lots of friends who are turkeys
Dey all hav a right to a life,
Not to be caged up an genetically made up
By any farmer an his wife.

Turkeys jus wanna play reggae
Turkeys jus wanna hip-hop
Can yu imagine a nice young turkey saying,
'I cannot wait for de chop'?
Turkeys like getting presents, dey wanna
    watch christmas TV,
Turkeys hav brains an turkeys feel pain
In many ways like yu an me.

I once knew a turkey called
Turkey
He said 'Benji explain to me please,
Who put de turkey in christmas
An what happens to christmas trees?'
I said, 'I am not too sure turkey
But it's nothing to do wid Christ Mass
Humans get greedy an waste more dan need be
An business men mek loadsa cash.'

Be nice to yu turkey dis christmas
Invite dem indoors fe sum greens
Let dem eat cake an let dem partake
In a plate of organic grown beans,
Be nice to yu turkey dis christmas
An spare dem de cut of de knife,
Join Turkeys United an dey'll be delighted
An yu will mek new friends **'FOR LIFE'.**

Benjamin Zephaniah

The Tomcat

At midnight in the alley
A tomcat comes to wail,
And he chants the hate of a million years
As he swings his snaky tail.

Malevolent, bony, brindled,
Tiger and devil and bard,
His eyes are coals from the middle of hell
And his heart is black and hard.

He twists and crouches and capers
And bares his curved sharp claws,
And he sings to the stars of the jungle nights
Ere cities were, or laws.

Beast from a world primeval,
He and his leaping clan,
When the blotched red moon leers over the
     roofs,
Give voice to their scorn of man.

He will lie on a rug tomorrow
And lick his silky fur,
And veil the brute in his yellow eyes,
And play he's tame, and purr.

But at midnight in the alley
He will crouch again and wail,
And beat the time for his demon's song
With the swing of his demon's tail.

Don Marquis

Rat It Up

C'mon everybody
Slap some grease on those paws
Get some yellow on your teeth
And, uh, sharpen up your claws

There's a whole lot of sausage
We're gonna swallow down
We're going to jump out the sewers
And rock this town

   Cos we're ratting it up
   Yes we're ratting it up
   Well we're ratting it up
   For a ratting good time tonight

Ain't got no compass
You don't need no map
Just follow your snout
Hey, watch out for that trap!

You can take out a poodle
You can beat up a cat
But if you can't lick a ferret
You ain't no kind of rat

Cos we're ratting it up
Yes we're ratting it up
Well we're ratting it up
For a ratting good time tonight

Now you can sneak in the henhouse
Roll out the eggs
But if the farmer comes running
Bite his hairy legs

Check that cheese for poison
Before you eat
Or you'll wind up being served up
As ratburger meat

Cos we're ratting it up
Yes we're ratting it up
Well we're ratting it up
For a ratting good time tonight

This rat was born to rock
This rat was born to roll
I don't give a monkey's
Bout your pest control

So push off pussy-cat
Push off pup
We're the Rockin' Rodents
And we're ratting it up

Yeah we're ratting it up
Yeah we're ratting it up
Well we're ratting it up
For a ratting good time tonight!

Adrian Mitchell

Out in the City

When you're out in the city
Shuffling down the street,
A bouncy city rhythm
Starts to boogie in your feet.

It jumps off the pavement,
There's a snare drum in your brain,
It pumps through your heart
Like a diesel train.

There's Harry on the corner,
Sings, 'How she goin', boy?'
To loose and easy Winston
With his brother Leroy.

Shout, 'Hello!' to Billy Brisket
With his tripes and cows heels,
Blood-stained rabbits
And trays of live eels.

Maltese Tony
Smoking in the shade
Keeping one good eye
On the amusement arcade.

And everybody's talking:

Move along
Step this way
Here's a bargain
What you say?
Mind your backs
Here's your stop
More fares?
Room on top.

Neon lights and take-aways
Gangs of girls and boys
Football crowds and market stalls
Taxi cabs and noise.

From the city cafés
On the smoky breeze
Smells of Indian cooking
Greek and Cantonese.

Well, some people like suburban life
Some people like the sea
Others like the countryside
But it's the city
Yes it's the city
It's the city life
For me.

Gareth Owen

Gran Can You Rap?

Gran was in her chair she was taking a nap
When I tapped her on the shoulder to see if
  she could rap.
Gran, can you rap? Can you rap? Can you,
  Gran?
And she opened one eye and said to me, man,
  I'm the best rapping Gran this world's ever
    seen
  I'm a tip-top, slip-slap, rap-rap queen.

And she rose from her chair in the corner of
  the room
And she started to rap with a bim-bam-boom,
And she rolled up her eyes and she rolled
  round her head
And as she rolled by this is what she said,
  I'm the best rapping Gran this world's ever
    seen
  I'm a nip-nap, yip-yap, rap-rap queen.

Then she rapped past my dad and she rapped
    past my mother,
She rapped past me and my little baby
    brother.
She rapped her arms narrow she rapped her
    arms wide,
She rapped through the door and she rapped
    outside.
    She's the best rapping Gran this world's
        ever seen
    She's a drip-drop, trip-trap, rap-rap queen.

She rapped down the garden she rapped down
    the street,
The neighbours all cheered and they tapped
    their feet.
She rapped through the traffic lights as they
    turned red
As she rapped round the corner this is what
    she said,
    I'm the best rapping Gran this world's ever
        seen
    I'm a flip-flop, hip-hop, rap-rap queen.

She rapped down the lane she rapped up the
   hill,
And as she disappeared she was rapping still.
I could hear Gran's voice saying, Listen, man,
Listen to the rapping of the rap-rap Gran.

I'm the best rapping Gran this world's ever
   seen
I'm a—
   tip-top, slip-slap,
    nip-nap, yip-yap,
     hip-hop, trip-trap,
      touch yer cap,
       take a nap,
        happy, happy, happy, happy,
         rap—rap—queen.

Jack Ousbey

Children's Prayer

Let the teachers of our class
Set us tests that we all pass.
Let them never ever care
About what uniform we wear.
Let them always clearly state
It's OK if your homework's late.
Let them say it doesn't matter
When we want to talk and chatter.

Let our teachers shrug and grin
When we make an awful din.
Let them tell us every day
There are no lessons. Go and play.
Let them tell our mum and dad
We're always good and never bad.
Let them write in their report
We are the best class they have taught!

John Foster

Blame

Graham, look at Maureen's leg,
She says you tried to tattoo it!
I did, Miss, yes—with my biro,
But Jonathan told me to do it.

Graham, look at Peter's sock,
It's got a burn-hole through it!
It was just an experiment, Miss, with the lens.
Jonathan told me to do it.

Alice's bag is stuck to the floor,
Look, Graham, did you glue it?
Yes, but I never thought it would work,
And Jonathan told me to do it.

Jonathan, what's all this I hear
About you and Graham Prewitt?
Well, Miss, it's really more his fault:
He *tells* me to tell him to do it!

Allan Ahlberg

Excuses, Excuses

Late again, Blenkinsopp?
What's the excuse this time?
Not my fault, sir.
Whose fault is it then?
Grandma's, sir.
Grandma's? What did she do?
She died, sir.
Died?
She's seriously dead all right, sir.
That makes four grandmothers this term,
  Blenkinsopp
And all on P.E. days.
I know. It's very upsetting, sir.
How many grandmothers have you got,
  Blenkinsopp?
Grandmothers, sir? None, sir.
You said you had four.
All dead, sir.
And what about yesterday, Blenkinsopp?
What about yesterday, sir?
You were absent yesterday.
That was the dentist, sir.
The dentist died?
No, sir. My teeth, sir.
You missed the maths test, Blenkinsopp!
I'd been looking forward to it, sir.

Right, line up for P.E.
Can't, sir.
No such word as 'can't', Blenkinsopp.
No kit, sir.
Where is it?
Home, sir.
What's it doing at home?
Not ironed, sir.
Couldn't you iron it?
Can't, sir.
Why not?
Bad hand, sir.
Who usually does it?
Grandma, sir.
Why couldn't she do it?
Dead, sir.

Gareth Owen

What Did You Learn In School Today?

What did you learn in school today,
Dear little boy of mine?
What did you learn in school today,
Dear little boy of mine?
I learned that Washington never told a lie,
I learned that soldiers seldom die,
I learned that everybody's free,
That's what the teacher said to me,
And that's what I learned in school today,
That's what I learned in school.

What did you learn in school today,
Dear little boy of mine?
What did you learn in school today,
Dear little boy of mine?
I learned that policemen are my friends,
I learned that justice never ends,
I learned that murderers die for their crimes,
Even if we make a mistake sometimes,
And that's what I learned in school today,
That's what I learned in school.

What did you learn in school today,
Dear little boy of mine?
What did you learn in school today,
Dear little boy of mine?
I learned our government must be strong,
It's always right and never wrong,
Our leaders are the finest men,
And we elect them again and again,
And that's what I learned in school today,
That's what I learned in school.

What did you learn in school today,
Dear little boy of mine?
What did you learn in school today,
Dear little boy of mine?
I learned that war is not so bad,
I learned about the great ones we have had,
We fought in Germany and France,
And someday I might get my chance,
And that's what I learned in school today,
That's what I learned in school.

Tom Paxton

Nursery Rhyme of Innocence and Experience

I had a silver penny
  And an apricot tree
And I said to the sailor
  On the white quay

'Sailor O sailor
  Will you bring me
If I give you my penny
  And my apricot tree

'A fez from Algeria
  An Arab drum to beat
A little gilt sword
  And a parakeet?'

And he smiled and he kissed me
  As strong as death
And I saw his red tongue
  And I felt his sweet breath

*'You may keep your penny
  And your apricot tree
And I'll bring your presents
  Back from sea.'*

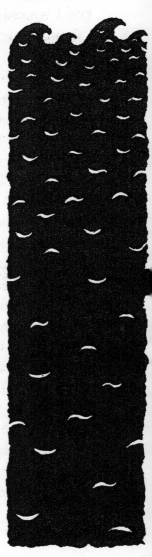

O the ship dipped down
  On the rim of the sky
And I waited while three
  Long summers went by

Then one steel morning
  On the white quay
I saw a grey ship
  Come in from sea

Slowly she came
  Across the bay
For her flashing rigging
  Was shot away

All round her wake
  The seabirds cried
And flew in and out
  Of the hole in her side

Slowly she came
  In the path of the sun
And I heard the sound
  Of a distant gun

And a stranger came running
    Up to me
From the deck of the ship
    And he said, said he

'O *are you the boy*
    Who would wait on the quay
With the silver penny
    And the apricot tree?

'*I've a plum-coloured fez*
    And a drum for thee
And a sword and a parakeet
    From over the sea.'

'O where is the sailor
    With bold red hair?
And what is that volley
    On the bright air?

'O where are the other
    Girls and boys?
And why have you brought me
    Children's toys?'

Charles Causley

O What is that Sound?

O what is that sound which so thrills the ear
   Down in the valley drumming, drumming?
Only the scarlet soldiers, dear,
   The soldiers coming.

O what is that light I see flashing so clear
   Over the distance brightly, brightly?
Only the sun on their weapons, dear,
   As they step lightly.

O what are they doing with all that gear;
   What are they doing this morning, this
 morning?
Only the usual manoeuvres, dear,
   Or perhaps a warning.

O why have they left the road down there;
   Why are they suddenly wheeling, wheeling?
Perhaps a change in the orders, dear;
   Why are you kneeling?

O haven't they stopped for the doctor's care;
   Haven't they reined their horses, their
 horses?
Why, they are none of them wounded, dear,
   None of these forces.

O is it the parson they want with white hair;
   Is it the parson, is it, is it?
No, they are passing his gateway, dear,
   Without a visit.

O it must be the farmer who lives so near;
   It must be the farmer so cunning, so
 cunning;
They have passed the farm already, dear,
   And now they are running.

O where are you going? stay with me here!
   Were the vows you swore me deceiving,
 deceiving?
No, I promised to love you, dear,
   But I must be leaving.

O it's broken the lock and splintered the door,
   O it's the gate where they're turning,
 turning;
Their feet are heavy on the floor
   And their eyes are burning.

W. H. Auden

Ballad of Birmingham
(Alabama)

'Mother, dear, may I go downtown
instead of out to play,
and march the streets of Birmingham
in a freedom march today?'

'No, baby, no, you may not go,
for the dogs are fierce and wild,
and clubs and hoses, guns and jails
ain't good for a little child.'

'But, mother, I won't be alone.
Other children will go with me,
and march the streets of Birmingham
to make our country free.'

'No, baby, no, you may not go,
for I fear those guns will fire.
But you may go to church instead,
and sing in the children's choir.'

She has combed and brushed her nightdark
  hair,
and bathed rose-petal sweet,
and drawn white gloves on her small brown
  hands,
and white shoes on her feet.

The mother smiled to know her child
was in the sacred place,
but that smile was the last smile
to come upon her face.

For when she heard the explosion,
her eyes grew wet and wild.
She raced through the streets of Birmingham
calling for her child.

She clawed through bits of glass and brick,
then lifted out a shoe.
'O, here's the shoe my baby wore,
but, baby, where are you?'

Dudley Randall

Tell Me Why?

Daddy will you tell me why
There are no battleships in the sky?
    The reason is apparently
    They only battle on the sea

Then will you tell me if you please
Why grandfather clocks cannot sneeze?
    The reason is, or so I'm told
    They're too stupid and too old

Will you explain once and for all
Why little Jack Horner fell off the wall?
    It wasn't him it was little Bo Peep
    Now be a good boy and go to sleep

Daddy will you tell me when
Little boys grow into men?
    Some never do that's why they fight
    Now kiss me, let me hold you tight

For in the morning I must go
To join my regiment and so
    For Queen and country bravely die
    Son, oh son, please tell me why?

Roger McGough

Icarus

Voice 1   Icarus, Icarus,
tell me why,
why did you fly
so high in the sky,
away from the cliff tops
and silent sea caves,
and over the restless,
murmuring waves?

Icarus   I flew to be free
like the birds
of the air.
I felt my wings ripple,
and shiver, and flare.
I felt the breeze rush
through my curly, black hair,
as I flew,
as I flew,
through the air.

Voice 2   Yes, you glided and swooped,
and you soared like a bird.
And your father was calling,
but you never heard.
For the beckoning sun
was golden and bright,

as you flew,
as you flew,
to the light.

Icarus   I was higher
than eagles
have ever dared fly,
when I saw feathers drifting
across the blue sky,
drifting like snow
to the waves far below.
And my father was calling,
calling, calling.
But I was already
falling, falling.

Voice 3   Icarus,
far below the green waves,
Icarus,
haunting the silent sea caves,
the sun cannot harm you
or dazzle your eyes,
as it did long ago
when you flew
through the skies,
through the burning,
blazing skies.

Voices 1, 2, 3	Then a sob
	like the murmur
	of rippling sea waves,
	echoes among
	the silent sea caves,
	as the ghost
	of Icarus
	sighs and says:

Icarus	Remember the boy
	who flew on the breeze
	away from the cliff tops
	and over the seas.
	Who dared
	to fly higher
	than eagles dare fly.
	Who tried to reach
	the sun in the sky.
	Remember the boy
	who longed
	to be free.
	Remember that boy . . .
	remember . . . me.

Cynthia Rider

The Legend of Ra and Isis of Ancient Egypt

Isis wished to become great and powerful,
a maker of things, a goddess of the earth
'Can I not become like Ra?' she asked
And so it was that Isis went to Ra
where he grew old and dribbled and slobbered
and Isis took that spit where it fell to the
  earth
and kneaded it and shaped it in her hands
till it became the snake.
And it came about that the snake bit Ra
and Ra came to Isis and spoke like this:
'As I went through the Two Lands of Egypt
looking over the world I have created,
something stung me
something, I know not what.

is it fire?
is it water?
I am colder than water
I am hotter than fire
my flesh sweats
I shake
what I see, fades in front of me
I can no longer see the sky itself

sweat rushes to my face
as if it were a summer's day'

Then Isis spoke to Ra:
'It is a snake that has bitten you:
a thing, that you, yourself, have created
has reared up its head against you?
I say to you,
it is my power, my words
that will drive out the poison of the snake
I will drive it from your sight
I will put it beyond the reach of the rays of
   the sun

So, godly father,
tell unto me, your secret name,
for if you want to live
it is your secret name that will save you.'

and Ra said
'I have made the skies and the earth
I have made the mountains
I have made all that is above them
I have made the great and wide sea
I have made the joys of love
I have stretched out the two horizons
like a curtain
and I have placed the gods there

when I open my eyes
I make light
when I close them
darkness comes.
The waters of the River Nile rise
when I say so
yet the gods themselves do not know
my secret name
I have made the hours

I have made the days
I have made the festivals of the year
I have made the floods of the River Nile
I have made fire
I provide food for the people in their houses

I am called Khepera in the morning
I am called Ra at midday
I am called Tmu in the evening'

But the poison did not leave the body of Ra
the poison bit into him deeper and deeper
and the great god could walk no more

Then Isis said to Ra
'But you have not said your secret name
Tell it me now

and the poison will flow from your body
for he who tells his secret name
will live.'

Now the poison burned like fire
fiercer even than a flame
fiercer even than a furnace
and so the great god said
'I will allow you, Isis
to search into me
so that my secret name can pass from me to
   you.'

Then the great god hid himself
from the other gods
and his place in the Boat of a Million Years
   was empty

The secret name of the great god, Ra
was taken from him
and Isis the maker of magic
said,
'Poison go!
Flow from Ra now!

It is my magic that moves
It is I
who can make the poison surrender
and flow out on to the earth

Ra live!
Poison die!
Poison die!
Ra live!
These are my words, I am
Isis, the great goddess
the queen of the gods
the one and only
who knows Ra by his secret name.'

Michael Rosen

How the Tortoise Got Its Shell

Come to my feast!
cried the great god Zeus.
Today I shall be wed!
And from each corner of the earth
all Zeus's creatures sped . . .

The fliers and the creepers,
the long, the short, the tall;
the crawlers and the leapers,
the feathered, furred, and bald;
hunters, biters, finders, fighters,
hooters, whistlers, roarers;
squeakers, screamers, squawkers, dreamers,
nibblers, gulpers, borers.
Paws and claws from hills and shores
from south, from north, from west and east,
from mountain tops and forest floors
all Zeus's creatures joined the feast
except
       the tortoise

They raved, they pranced, they feasted,
   danced;
six days and nights each creature stayed
to chatter, flatter, clap, and cheer
at the great god Zeus's grand parade
except
         the tortoise.

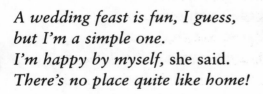

Next day . . .
Why weren't you there, my friend, asked
   Zeus,
the day that I was wed?

The tortoise smiled her small, slow smile
and raised her small, slow head.

A wedding feast is fun, I guess,
but I'm a simple one.
I'm happy by myself, she said.
There's no place quite like home!

How dare you stay away! roared Zeus.
I'll show you just what for!
From this day on you'll carry your home
on your back, for evermore!

Judith Nicholls

57

Get Up and Shut the Door

It happened one December night,
   And a dark night it was then,
That an old wife had puddings to make:
   She boiled them in the pan.

The wind blew cold from south and north.
   It blew across the floor:
The old man said to his old wife,
   'Get up and shut the door.'

'My hands are in the pudding basin.
   Husband, can't you see?
If it has to wait a hundred years,
   It won't be shut by me.'

They made a pact between the two.
   They made it firm and sure:
'The one who is the first to speak
   Gets up and shuts the door.'

Two gentlemen came passing by
    At twelve o'clock that night.
They couldn't see the house at all.
    Nor coal, nor candle-light.

They hit the house. 'May we come in?
    Is anyone there?' they cried.
And then they went in through the door,
    For no one had replied.

First they ate the white puddings,
    Then they ate the black;
But never a word the old wife spoke,
    Though she was hopping mad.

Then one man said to the other man,
    'Here now! Take my knife.
You cut off the old man's beard,
    And I will kiss his wife.'

'But there's no water in the house,
    So what shall we do then?'
'You'll have to use the pudding water
    Boiling in the pan.'

Then up sprang the old man,
    An angry man was he:
'What! Kiss my wife before my face
    And slop that muck on me?'

Then up sprang the old wife
    And gave three skips on the floor:
'Husband, you were the first to speak:
    Get up and shut the door.'

Ian Serraillier

A Smuggler's Song

If you wake at midnight, and hear a horse's
  feet,
Don't go drawing back the blind, or looking
  in the street.
Them that asks no questions isn't told a lie.
Watch the wall, my darling, while the
  Gentlemen go by!

      Five and twenty ponies,
      Trotting through the dark—
      Brandy for the Parson,
      'Baccy for the Clerk;
      Laces for a lady, letters for a spy,
And watch the wall, my darling, while the
  Gentlemen go by!

Running round the woodlump if you chance
  to find
Little barrels, roped and tarred, all full of
  brandy-wine,
Don't you shout to come and look, nor use
  'em for your play.
Put the brushwood back again—and they'll be
  gone next day!

If you see a stable-door setting open wide;
If you see a tired horse lying down inside;
If your mother mends a coat cut about and
tore;
If the lining's wet and warm—don't you ask
no more!

If you meet King George's men, dressed in
blue and red,
You be careful what you say, and mindful
what is said.
If they call you 'pretty maid', and chuck you
'neath the chin,
Don't you tell where no one is, nor yet where
no one's been!

Knocks and footsteps round the house—
whistles after dark—
You've no call for running out till the house-
dogs bark.
Trusty's here, and Pincher's here, and see how
dumb they lie—
They don't fret to follow when the Gentlemen
go by!

If you do as you've been told, 'likely there's a
  chance,
You'll be give a dainty doll, all the way from
  France,
With a cap of Valenciennes, and a velvet
  hood—
A present from the Gentlemen, along o' being
  good!
  Five and twenty ponies,
  Trotting through the dark—
  Brandy for the Parson,
  'Baccy for the Clerk.
Them that asks no questions isn't told a lie—
Watch the wall, my darling, while the
  Gentlemen go by!

Rudyard Kipling

The Listeners

'Is there anybody there?' said the Traveller,
  Knocking on the moonlit door;
And his horse in the silence champed the grasses
  Of the forest's ferny floor:
And a bird flew up out of the turret,
  Above the Traveller's head:
And he smote upon the door again a second
  time;
  'Is there anybody there?' he said.
But no one descended to the Traveller;
  No head from the leaf-fringed sill
Leaned over and looked into his grey eyes,
  Where he stood perplexed and still.
But only a host of phantom listeners
  That dwelt in the lone house then
Stood listening in the quiet of the moonlight
  To that voice from the world of men:
Stood thronging the faint moonbeams on the
  dark stair,
  That goes down to the empty hall,
Hearkening in an air stirred and shaken
  By the lonely Traveller's call.
And he felt in his heart their strangeness,
  Their stillness answering his cry,
While his horse moved, cropping the dark turf,
  'Neath the starred and leafy sky;

For he suddenly smote on the door, even
  Louder, and lifted his head:—
'Tell them I came, and no one answered,
  That I kept my word,' he said.
Never the least stir made the listeners,
  Though every word he spake
Fell echoing through the shadowiness of the
  still house
  From the one man left awake:
Ay, they heard his foot upon the stirrup,
  And the sound of iron on stone,
And how the silence surged softly backward,
  When the plunging hoofs were gone.

Walter de la Mare

The Headless Horseman

The headless horseman rides tonight
through stark and starless skies.
Shattering the silence
with his otherwordly cries,
he races through the darkness
on his alabaster steed.
The headless horseman rides tonight
wherever the fates would lead.

And he rides upon the wind tonight,
he rides upon the wind,
galloping, galloping, galloping on
out of the great oblivion,
galloping till the night is gone,
he rides upon the wind tonight,
he rides upon the wind.

The headless horseman rides tonight
begarbed in robes of black
to bear a being from the earth
never to bring him back.
He is evil's foul embodiment,
with laughter on his breath.
The headless horseman rides tonight,
the minister of death.

And he rides upon the wind tonight,
he rides upon the wind,
galloping, galloping, galloping on
out of the great oblivion,
galloping till the night is gone,
he rides upon the wind tonight,
he rides upon the wind.

The headless horseman rides tonight,
he rides the wind alone.
Beneath his arm he tightly tucks
his head of gleaming bone.
His voice is harsh and hollow,
it is horrible to hear.
The headless horseman rides tonight
to fill the earth with fear.

And he rides upon the wind tonight,
he rides upon the wind,
galloping, galloping, galloping on
out of the great oblivion,
galloping till the night is gone,
he rides upon the wind tonight,
he rides upon the wind.

The headless horseman rides tonight
upon his fateful trip.
With silvery scythe of steely death
held fast in bony grip,
he sweeps it swiftly forth and back
as over the earth he glides.
And none in the world is safe tonight
for the headless horseman rides.

And he rides upon the wind tonight,
he rides upon the wind,
galloping, galloping, galloping on
out of the great oblivion,
galloping till the night is gone,
he rides upon the wind tonight,
he rides upon the wind.

Jack Prelutsky

Let Us In

'Let us in! Let us in!'
Who is crying above the wind's din?

'Let us in! Let us in!
We are pale and cold and thin.'

A clock chimes the midnight hour.
Are they creatures with magic power?

'Let us in! Let us in!
We are pale and cold and thin.'

They come and come and more and more.
Close the curtains! Lock the door!

'Let us in! Let us in!
We are pale and cold and thin.'

'Let us in! Let us in!
We are pale and cold and thin.'

Olive Dove

Ghosts' Boasts

'I've found out about walking through walls;
I did it a lot tonight.'

'I've been able to do that for ages.
Can you glow with an unearthly light?'

'Yes—and make the light change colour:
First white, then pale green, then red.'

'I can do all those—and purple.
Do you know how to take off your head?'

'That's simple! I carry it—screaming—
In my hands or under my arm.'

'Sounds great! Any more tricks
To spread panic and fear and alarm?'

'Lots: clanking chains, dreadful laughs
And evil, staring eyes . . .'

'That all sounds a bit fantastic;
Are you sure you're not telling lies?'

'Well, you're the one who began it
With that really stupid boast . . .'

'Sorry—I suppose the truth is
I'm just not a successful ghost.
Whenever I try out something haunting,
Some new tricks . . . I don't know about you . . .
I've not scared a mortal for ages.
They all laugh at me.'

'And at me too.'

Eric Finney

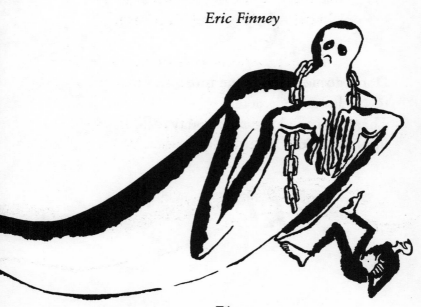

71

Nightmare Cemetery

Don't go down with me today
to Nightmare Cemetery
You don't know what you'll see today
in Nightmare Cemetery

Don't go through the gates today
to Nightmare Cemetery
You don't know what waits today
in Nightmare Cemetery

Don't go down the lane today
to Nightmare Cemetery
There you might remain today
in Nightmare Cemetery

Don't go down the road today
to Nightmare Cemetery
Haunt of bat and toad today
in Nightmare Cemetery

The sun will never shine today
in Nightmare Cemetery
Horrors wait in line today
in Nightmare Cemetery

Close the gates and step inside
Much too late to try and hide
Hear the hinges creak with glee
I'll be waiting, just you see,
You're here forever, just like me
in Nightmare Cemetery.

Adrian Henri

Owl

'Who?
Who are you?
Who?'

      'I am owl,
      night's eyes,
      wise beyond understanding.'

'Who?
Who are you?
Who?'

      'I am owl,
      shadow of shadows,
      owner of forests,
      beautiful beyond comprehension.'

'Who?
Who are you?
Who?'

      'I am owl,
      plucker of moonbeams,
      owl, most mysterious.
      Beware.'

Patricia Hubbell

This is a Rune I Have Heard a Tree Say

This is a rune I have heard a tree say:
'Love me. I cannot run away.'

This is a rune I have heard a lark cry:
'So high! But I cannot reach the sky.'

This is a rune I have heard a dog bark:
'I see what is not even there in the dark.'

This is a rune I have heard a fish weep:
'I am trying to find you when I leap.'

This is a rune I have heard a cat miaow:
'I died eight times so be kind to me now.'

This is a rune I have heard a man say:
'Hold your head up and you see far away.'

George Barker

The Wind

I can get through a doorway without any key,
And strip the leaves from the great oak tree.
I can drive storm-clouds and shake tall towers,
Or steal through a garden and not wake the
    flowers.
Seas I can move and ships I can sink;
I can carry a house-top or the scent of a pink.
When I am angry I can rave and riot;
And when I am spent, I lie quiet as quiet.

James Reeves

The Rain

I don't care what you say
I like
the rain,
I like it chucked like nails
against my win-
dow pane.

I don't care what you say
I like
the soak
of drizzle when it drifts
about the hills
like smoke.

I don't care what you say
I like
the flood
that makes our road the Nile
and leaves our lawn
all mud.

I don't care what you say
I like
it, so,
with hat and coat and yellow wellies, here
I go

on holiday to find
that fam-
ous plain
in Spain. I don't care what
you say, my friend,
I like
the rain.

Richard Edwards

from The Cloud

I bring fresh showers for the thirsting flowers,
    From the seas and the streams;
I bear light shade for the leaves when laid
    In their noonday dreams.
From my wings are shaken the dews that waken
    The sweet buds every one,
When rocked to rest on their mother's breast,
    As she dances about the sun.
I wield the flail of the lashing hail,
    And whiten the green plains under,
And then again I dissolve it in rain,
    And laugh as I pass in thunder.

Percy Bysshe Shelley

River Song

'Oh where are you going?' said Rover to river,
'You flow always downward. Why should that
   be?'
'I gather the droplets of water together
And carry them home to their mother, the sea.'

'From moment to moment,' said Rover to
   river,
'Your waters are changing, yet you stay the
   same.'
'No. I am the mocker of every map-maker;
Although they outline me and give me a
   name.'

'I'm banked and I'm bridged,' said river to
   Rover.
'I'm built by; I'm fished in, I'm wished on as
   well.
But I am a winder; I love to wander.
Every day I am different, with stories to tell,'

'Of floods and disasters,' said river to Rover,
'Of long lazy summers, of ducks in my weeds,
Of wild otter huntings, of strange ghostly
   hauntings,
Of crisp frozen winters with ice on my reeds.'

'Of towns that surround me,' said river to
  Rover,
'Until I escape through the bridges, to fields
Where brown cattle wallow beside my green
  willows,
And small beetles strut, with their bright
  shining shields.'

'And all the time downward,' said river to
  Rover,
'I travel past building and boulder and tree.
I gather the driplets and droplets together
And hurry them home to their mother, the
  sea.'

Gerard Benson

Old Man Ocean

Old Man Ocean, how do you pound
Smooth glass rough, rough stones round?
  *Time and the tide and the wild waves
  rolling.*
  *Night and the wind and the long grey
  dawn.*

Old Man Ocean, what do you tell,
What do you sing in the empty shell?
  Fog and storm and the long bell tolling,
  Bones in the deep and the brave men gone.

Russell Hoban

Seasons

Every season has its reason:
Summer, Autumn, Winter, Spring.
There is a kind of rhyme in time
For what will grow and who shall sing.

I am Summer. My shimmering sun
Glimmers with gold the streams that run
Through deep-green hills. And butterflies
Float petal-like on bold blue skies.

I am Autumn, called sometimes Fall,
When frail leaves shawl each lawn and wall;
When morning's wrapped in lacy mist,
And rosy apples fill the fist.

I am Winter, sharp, severe.
I nip at nose and toes and ear.
I carpet roads with ice and snow
While small birds seek red berries' glow.

I am Spring, royal, richly green,
When bright birds sing; new buds are seen;
When silly lambs cram fields and roads,
And tadpoles magic strangely into toads.

Every season has its reason:
Summer, Autumn, Winter, Spring.
There is a kind of rhyme in time
For what will grow and who shall sing.

John Kitching

Autumn News Bulletin

Today, the trees are in shock.
Overnight, a sustained assault
Has left them battered and bare.
There are leaves everywhere—
On roads and pathways,
Scattered on lawns and flowerbeds,
Clustered in doorways
And the corners of buildings.

In some gardens
Men with rakes have appeared.
In due course, barrow-loads of leaves
Will be heaped into bonfires.
Now, in the aftermath of the storm,
There is an air of resignation.
As one of the residents put it:
'I suppose it's to be expected.
It happens every year.'

John Foster

The Shepherd's Carol

We stood on the hills, Lady,
Our day's work done,
Watching the frosted meadows
That winter had won.

The evening was calm, Lady,
The air so still,
Silence more lovely than music
Folded the hill.

There was a star, Lady,
Shone in the night,
Larger than Venus it was
And bright, so bright.

Oh, a voice from the sky, Lady,
It seemed to us then
Telling of God being born
In the world of men.

And so we have come, Lady,
Our day's work done,
Our love, our hopes, ourselves
We give to your son

Anon.

Poor Man

What have you got to eat,

                   poor man?

   Nothing, he said,
   But a crust of bread,
A crust that is shared is sweet,

                   poor man.

What sort of roof have you,

                   poor man?

   Nothing, he said
   But a shepherd's shed.
A shed that takes one takes two,

                   poor man.

What can you give your wife,

                   poor man?

   Nothing, he said,
   But hand, heart, and head.
It's a gift that will last for life,

                   poor man.

Eleanor Farjeon

'I,' said the Donkey

'I,' said the donkey, all shaggy and brown,
'Carried his mother all into the town,
Carried her uphill, carried her down,
I,' said the donkey, all shaggy and brown.

'I,' said the cow, with spots of red,
'Gave him hay for to rest his head,
Gave him a manger for his bed.
I,' said the cow with spots of red.

'I,' said the sheep, with twisted horn,
'Gave my wool for to keep him warm,
Gave my coat on Christmas morn.
I,' said the sheep with twisted horn.

'I,' said the dove from the rafters high,
'Cooed him to sleep with a lullaby,
Cooed him to sleep my mate and I.
I,' said the dove from the rafters high.

Anon.

Uphill

Does the road wind uphill all the way?
    Yes, to the very end.
Will the day's journey take the whole long
    day?
    From morn to night, my friend.

But is there for the night a resting-place?
    A roof for when the slow, dark hours begin.
May not the darkness hide it from my face?
    You cannot miss that inn.

Shall I meet other wayfarers at night?
    Those who have gone before
Then must I knock, or call when just in sight?
    They will not keep you waiting at that
    door.

Shall I find comfort, travel-sore and weak?
    Of labour you shall find the sum.
Will there be beds for me and all who seek?
    Yea, beds for all who come.

Christina Rossetti

The Splendour Falls on Castle Walls

The splendour falls on castle walls
   And snowy summits old in story:
The long light shakes across the lakes,
   And the wild cataract leaps in glory.
Blow, bugle, blow, set the wild echoes flying,
Blow, bugle; answer, echoes, dying, dying,
  dying.

O hark, O hear! how thin and clear,
   And thinner, clearer, farther, going!
O sweet and far from cliff and scar
   The horns of Elfland faintly blowing!
Blow, let us hear the purple glens replying:
Blow, bugle; answer, echoes, dying, dying,
  dying.

O love, they die in yon rich sky,
   They faint on hill or field or river:
Our echoes roll from soul to soul,
   And grow for ever and for ever.
Blow, bugle, blow, set the wild echoes flying,
And answer, echoes, answer, dying, dying,
  dying.

Alfred, Lord Tennyson

Celebration Song

Can you hear the people singing?
Can you hear, can you hear?
Can you hear the drummers drumming
as they go?
Can you see the flags a-flying
bright and clear, bright and clear
as they wave to all the children
down below?

It's a day of celebration—
yes it is, yes it is!
We should all of us be dancing
heel and toe,
for the time is come for caring
and the harvest is for sharing
and there's something there for everyone,
I know.

Now the babies will be feeding,
and the children all are reading
in a way they never learned to do
before,
and the homeless and forsaken
to new ways of life are taken,
and the sad ones will not suffer
any more
      any more—
            No, the sad ones will not suffer
                any more.

Jean Kenward

Index of titles and first lines
(First lines are in italic)

Index of authors

John Agard: 'The Spiders Cast Their Spell' reprinted from *We Animals Would Like a Word With You* (Bodley Head, 1996), copyright © John Agard 1996, by permission of the Random House Group Ltd. **Allan Ahlberg:** 'Blame' reprinted from *Please Mrs Butler* (Kestrel, 1983), copyright © Allan Ahlberg 1983, by permission of Penguin Books Ltd. **W. H. Auden:** 'O What is That Sound?', copyright 1937 and © renewed 1965 by W. H. Auden, reprinted from *Collected Poems* by permission of the publishers, Faber & Faber Ltd and Random House, Inc. **George Barker:** 'This is a rune I have heard a tree say' reprinted from *Runes and Rhymes and Tunes and Chimes* (1968) by permission of the publisher, Faber & Faber Ltd. **Gerard Benson:** 'River Song' reprinted from *Evidence of Elephants* (Viking, 1995, Smith-Doorstep, 2001), by permission of the author. **Charles Causley:** 'Nursery Rhyme of Innocence and Experience' reprinted from *Collected Poems 1951-2000* (Macmillan), by permission of David Higham Associates. **Walter de la Mare:** 'The Listeners' reprinted from *The Complete Poems of Walter de la Mare* (1969), by permission of The Literary Trustees of Walter de la Mare, and the Society of Authors as their representative. **Olive Dove:** 'Let us In', reprinted by permission of Mrs Ruth Dean. **Richard Edwards:** 'The Rain' reprinted from *Whispers from a Wardrobe* (Lutterworth, 1987) by permission of the author. **Eleanor Farjeon:** 'Poor Man' reprinted from *Something I Remember* (Blackie, 1987) by permission of David Higham Associates. **Eric Finney:** 'Ghosts' Boasts', copyright © Eric Finney 2001, first published in this collection by permission of the author. **Michael Flanders:** 'The Hippopotamus Song', words by Michael Flanders, music by Donald Swan, copyright © 1952 Warner/Chappell Music Ltd, London W6 8BS, reprinted by permission of International Music Publications Ltd. **John Foster:** 'Autumn News Bulletin' and 'Children's Prayer', copyright © John Foster 2001, first published in this collection by permission of the author. **Adrian Henri:** 'Nightmare Cemetery' reprinted from *The Phantom Lollipop Lady* (Methuen, 1986), copyright © Adrian Henri 1986, by permission of the author, c/o Rogers, Coleridge & White Ltd, 20 Powis Mews, London W11 1JN. **Russell Hoban:** 'Old Man Ocean' reprinted from *The Pedalling Man* (Heinemann, 1968) by permission of David Higham Associates. **Julie Holder:** 'The House of the Tiger' first published in John Foster (ed): *Face the Front* (OUP, 1994), reprinted by permission of the author. **Patricia Hubbell:** 'Owl' reprinted from *Catch Me a Wind* (Atheneum), copyright © 1968, 1994 Patricia Hubbell, by permission of Marian Reiner for the author. **Jean Kenward:** 'Celebration Song', copyright Jean Kenward 1992, first published in *Can you Hear? Poems for Oxfam* (Pan Macmillan, 1992), reprinted by permission of the author. **Rudyard Kipling:** 'A Smuggler's Song' reprinted from *Puck of Pook's Hill*, by Permission of A P Watt on behalf of The National Trust for Places of Historical Interest or Natural Beauty. **John Kitching:** 'Seasons', copyright © John Kitching 2001, first published in this collection by permission of the author. **Roger McGough:** 'Tell Me Why?' reprinted from *Sky in the Pie* (Kestrel, 1983), copyright Roger McGough 1983, by permission of PFD on behalf of Roger McGough. **Don Marquis:** 'The Tomcat' reprinted from *Poems and Portraits* (Doubleday, 1922), by permission of Doubleday, a division of Random House, Inc. **Adrian Mitchell:** 'Rat It Up' reprinted from *Balloon Lagoon and the Magic Islands of Poetry* (Orchard Books, 1997), copyright © Adrian Mitchell 1997, by permission of PFD on behalf of Adrian Mitchell. Educational Health Warning! Adrian Mitchell asks that none of his poems are used in connection with any examinations whatsoever. **Tony Mitton:** 'Song of the Wizard's Imp' reprinted from *Plum* (Scholastic Children's Books, 1998) by permission of David Higham Associates. **Grace Nichols:** 'I Am a Parrot' reprinted from *Come On Into My Tropical Garden* (A & C Black, 1988), copyright © Grace Nichols 1988, by permission of Curtis Brown Ltd, London on behalf of Grace Nichols. **Judith Nicholls:** 'How the Tortoise Got its Shell', copyright © Judith Nicholls 1995, reprinted from *Animal Lore* (Ginn, 1995), by permission of the author. **Jack Ousbey:** 'Gran Can You Rap?', copyright © Jack Ousbey 1993, first published in John Foster (ed): *All in the Family* (OUP, 1993) reprinted by permission of the author. **Gareth Owen:** 'Excuses, Excuses' and 'Out in the City' reprinted from *Collected Poems* (Macmillan, 2000) by permission of the author. **Brian Patten:** 'The Newcomer' reprinted from *Gargling with Jelly* (Viking Kestrel, 1985), copyright © Brian Patten 1985, by permission of Penguin Books Ltd and the author, c/o Rogers, Coleridge & White Ltd, 20 Powis Mews, London W11 1JN. **Jack Prelutsky:** 'The Headless Horseman' reprinted from *The Headless Horseman Rides Tonight* (Greenwillow Books, 1980, and A & C Black, 1984), text copyright © 1980 by Jack Prelutsky, by permission of the publishers, A & C Black (Publishers) Ltd and HarperCollins Publishers, Inc. **James Reeves:** 'The Wind' reprinted from *The Complete Poems for Children* (Heinemann, 1973), copyright © James Reeves 1973, by permission of the James Reeves Estate, c/o Laura Cecil Literary Agency. **Cynthia Rider:** 'Icarus', copyright © Cynthia Rider 2001, first published in this collection by permission of the author. **Michael Rosen:** 'The Legend of Ra and Isis of Ancient Egypt' reprinted from Michael Rosen (ed): *The Kingfisher Book of Children's Poetry* (1985), copyright © Michael Rosen 1985, by permission of PFD on behalf of Michael Rosen. **Andrew Salkey:** 'Anancy' first published in Gillian Clarke (ed): *The Whispering Room* (Kingfisher), reprinted by permission of Patricia Salkey. **Ian Serraillier:** 'Get Up and Shut the Door' reprinted from *I'll Tell You a Tale* (Longman 1973), copyright © Ian Serraillier 1973, by permission of Anne Serraillier. **Jennifer Tweedie:** 'Mang, Katong and the Crocodile King', copyright © Jennifer Tweedie 1997, first published in John Foster (ed): *Magic Poems* (OUP, 1997), reprinted by permission of the author. **Benjamin Zephaniah:** 'Talking Turkeys' reprinted from *Talking Turkeys* (Viking, 1994), copyright © Benjamin Zephaniah 1994, by permission of Penguin Books Ltd.

Despite every effort to try to trace and contact copyright holders before publication this has not been possible in every case. If notified the publisher will be pleased to rectify any errors or omissions at the earliest opportunity.